DEATHLY
HALLOWS
PART 1

Selections from

Harry Potter
AND THE
Deathly Hallows
PART I

Music by BY ALEXANDRE DESPLAT
Arranged by Dan Coates

CONTENTS

Produced by
Alfred Music Publishing Co., Inc.
P.O. Box 10003
Van Nuys, CA 91410-0003
alfred.com

ISBN-10: 0-7390-7775-9
ISBN-13: 978-0-7390-7775-7

OBLIVIATE

By Alexandre Desplat
Arranged by Dan Coates

Moderately slow (♩ = 76)

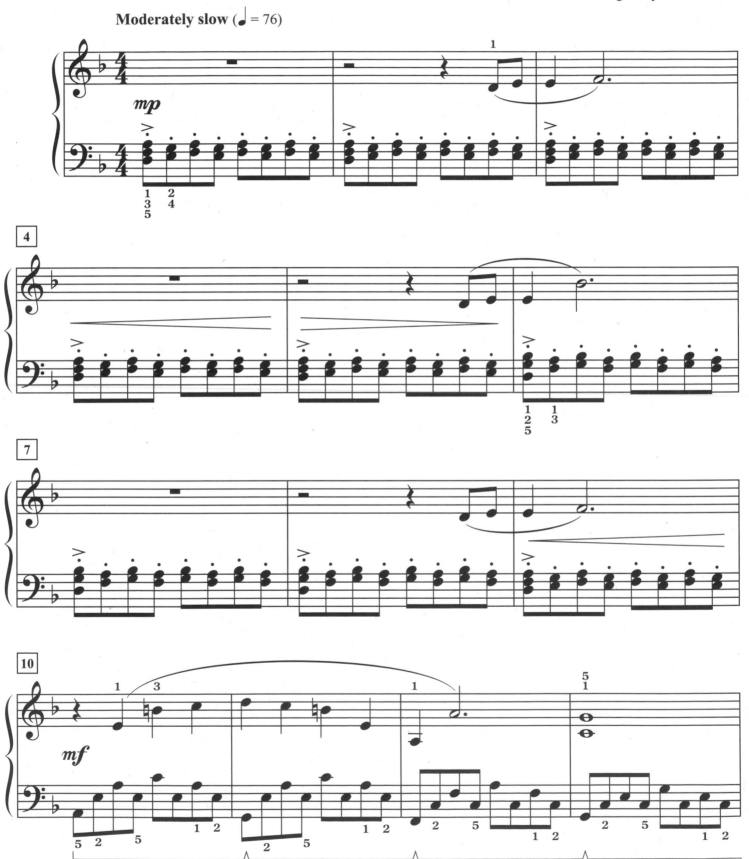

SNAPE TO MALFOY MANOR

By Alexandre Desplat
Arranged by Dan Coates

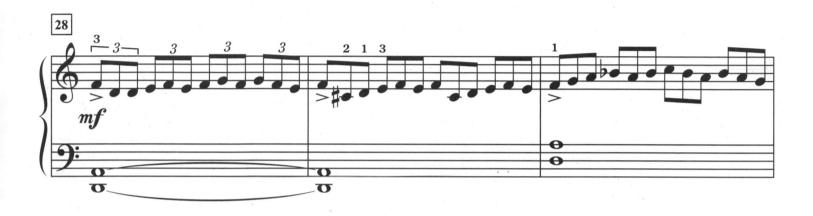

POLYJUICE POTION

By Alexandre Desplat
Arranged by Dan Coates

AT THE BURROW

By Alexandre Desplat
Arranged by Dan Coates

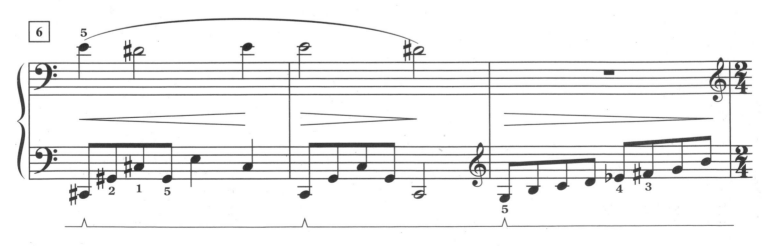

HARRY AND GINNY

By Alexandre Desplat
Arranged by Dan Coates

Slowly and tenderly ($\quad$ = 80)

RON LEAVES

By Alexandre Desplat
Arranged by Dan Coates

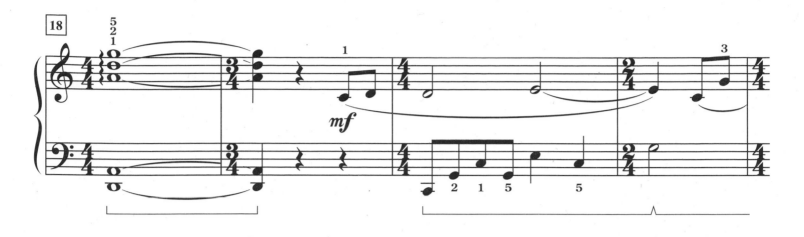

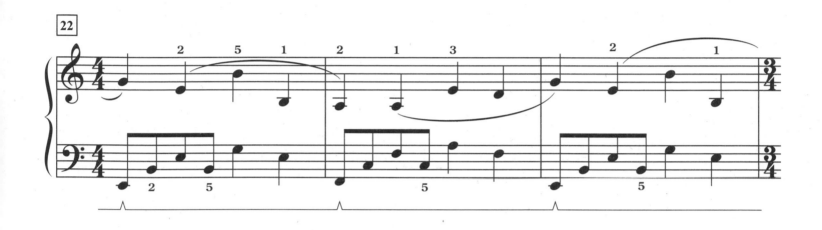

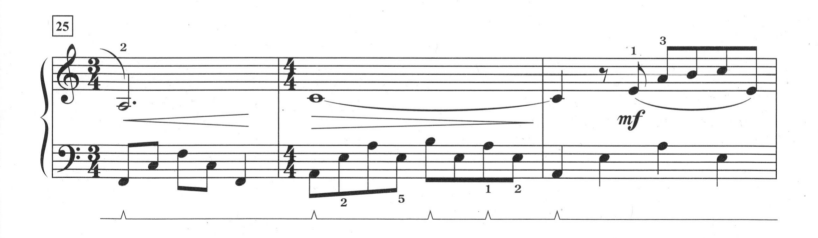

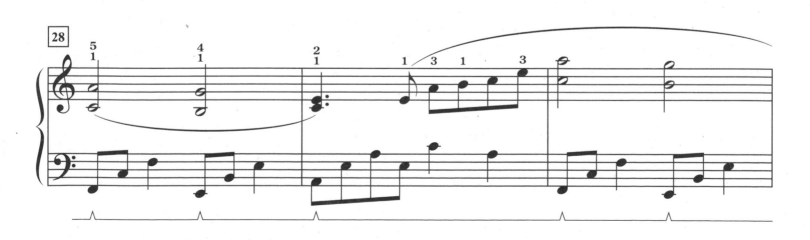

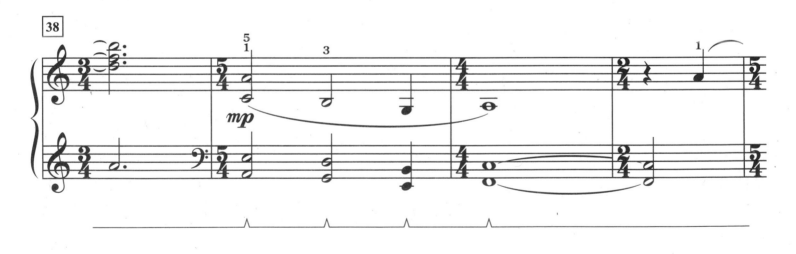

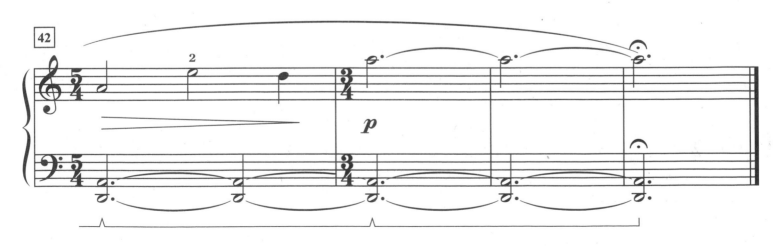

GODRIC'S HOLLOW GRAVEYARD

By Alexandre Desplat
Arranged by Dan Coates

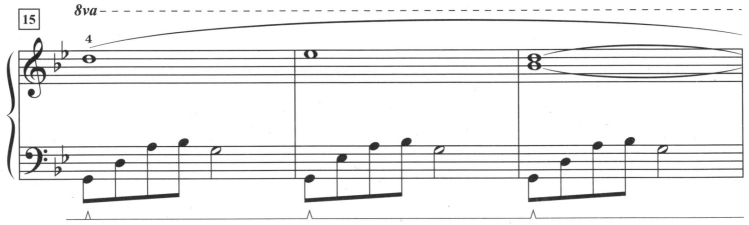

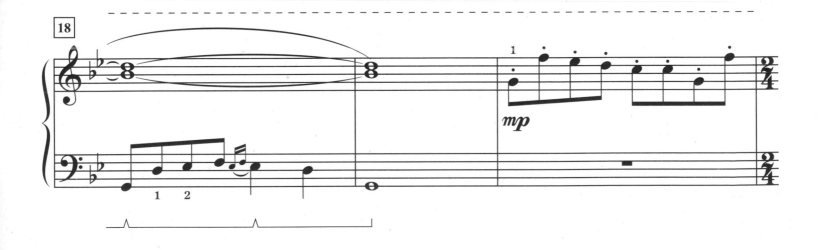

RON'S SPEECH

By Alexandre Desplat
Arranged by Dan Coates

LOVEGOOD

By Alexandre Desplat
Arranged by Dan Coates

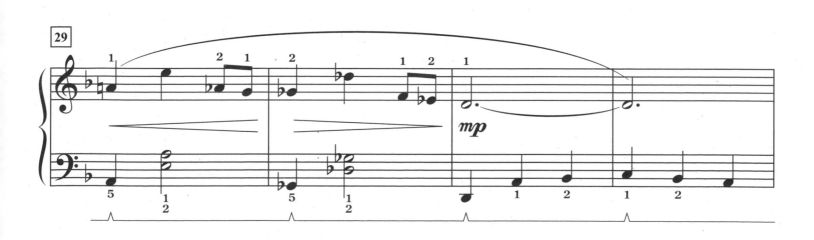

FAREWELL TO DOBBY

By Alexandre Desplat
Arranged by Dan Coates

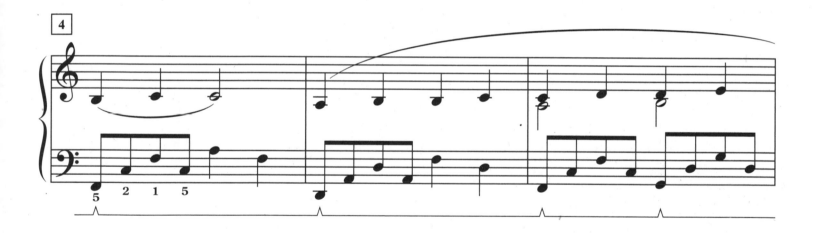